My Heart Open

Wendelyn Vega

Published by Wendelyn Vega, 2024.

While every precaution has been taken in the preparation of this book, the publisher assumes no responsibility for errors or omissions, or for damages resulting from the use of the information contained herein.

MY HEART OPEN

First edition. April 23, 2024.

Copyright © 2024 Wendelyn Vega.

Written by Wendelyn Vega.

For all hearts, broken and otherwise.

Lovely

Am I lovely?
I want to know.
Am I captivating
Wherever I go?
I put on my makeup.
I straighten my smile.
I try to loose weight.
I improve on my style.
Do you see beauty
When you look at me?
Do you think I'm special,
As good as can be?
I try to be better,
Demure and polite.
Coy and alluring,
Doing everything right.
But sometimes I fail,
I don't like what I see.
When I look in the mirror,
What I look at is me.
I'm not desirable,
And I'm not good.
I want to be perfect,
But I don't think I could.
Am I lovely?
Tell me the truth now.
I'll try to do better

If you'll tell me how.
I want to be wanted;
I need to be me.
I am a woman,
And I'm human, you see.

Myself

You don't have to like you to love you
They say.
I know.
But what if I want to?

Move on

Where does the pain go
When the storm is done?
Does it dissipate on the wind
Like the rain and tears,
Or do we paint it over
With a new color
And move on?

Catching Up

If you ask me how I've been,
Should I tell you the truth?
That I've been
Fighting uphill battles,
Drawing oil from empty jars.
That I've been
Painting barren landscapes,
Weighing hope against cold stone.
That I've been
Juggling joys and sorrows,
Playing catch up with my dreams.
Or should I smile
And nod
And say I've been doing fine?

How to lose a friend

It's easy.
Just ensure that you
make every decision
in the best interest of yourself.
Soon you will have
No one but yourself
to care for.

There's no cure

If everyone's truly strange,
Dancing the edge of a knife,
Courting the end of the world,
Willing or not for the strife,
If everyone's truly strange,
Hallucinating their dreams,
Blind to the concept of truth,
Silencing all of their screams,
If everyone's truly strange,
Wishing on metal and gas,
Hoping our hope will return,
Praying for peace that won't pass,
Is anyone truly strange?
Maybe we're already sure,
But if we're honest about that
We'll have to admit there's no cure.

Why must I be gracious

Why must I be gracious
As I'm cast by the side of the road,
Rejected? Abandoned
on the island of misfit toys
too bizarre to be loved.
When you say
"You are nice
but not worth it,"
Why must I smile and say "Thank you"
when you wouldn't do the same?

Ah yes, dating

It's no better or worse than it used to be.
If I could just stop banging my head against this wall for a moment
I would tell you...
Hang on, my phone just beeped.
There must be a new torment waiting for me.

Talking with strangers

They say
Butterflies in your belly
Means love,
But what does it mean
When they're trapped in your chest,
Keeping your clammy hands
From pressing "call"?

Arrow in My Heart

Arrow in my heart,
The wound has healed around you.
No more the constant throbbing,
just an often present lull.
But every now and then
your "still-there" tip, now dull,
will twist even a little
and the ache begins again.
I am well aware that the hurt
will wax and wane.
Still I must admit
It is a beautiful pain.

Sight

I love how your eyes change color,
shifting from forest to sky,
sometimes darkened with clouds,
but usually somewhere between.
I see you in turquoise gems
and crystal clear banks of snow,
sometimes a flushed red beet
but usually somewhere between.

I write words on your back

I write words on your back
That I know you can't read.
The tips of my fingers
Must tell you anyway
That when I vowed my all,
That I meant what I said,
That the words each still mean
What they did when we met.
That when moments are high
And when moments are low
That my hand's still in yours
Wherever we may tread.
I write words on your back
That I know you can't read.
The tips of my fingers
Must tell you anyway.

You are a song

You are a song inside my mind,
Enchanting in the cold.
Look at me with a lover's eyes—
Share in the warmth I hold.
I am an anchor keeping you
At home within the snow.
Stay with me as the fire dies
And bask in the ember's glow.

Thirteen Hearts

She holds thirteen hearts in
her hands
have seen pain and love
sadness and joy
tears and laughter in the lines of
her hands
have touched hundreds of lives
embraced hurting souls with
proof of God's comfort and will in the lines of
her hands
hold the proof and the love and
She holds thirteen hearts in
her hands

No one recovers

No one recovers from a broken heart.
We are made whole by collecting each part,
Putting the pieces in order and such,
Holding together when it gets too much.
Dusting the fragments of old selves with care
Filling the cracks that show off signs of wear.
We pour from the gold forged in our own fires.
We all grieve forever; some are just good liars.

Illustrious

You are a precious shelter
Open arms, a listening ear
Under heaven's special call
Making memories, wiping tears
Every day, each smile, each laugh
A helping hand, a constant guide
Stands the straight and narrow path
Upward, higher, side by side
Richly you have blessed our lives
Every day, each smile, each tear
Under heaven's special call
Priceless love throughout each year

When you were gone

Once upon a time
You said we'd sit
In silence
when you were gone,
But I know
That you know
We all carry
Mirrors of mothers
Walking through earth.
You echo yours
As I echo mine,
Present and past
To eternity.
I dream of
Giving you gardens
While you are here.
Why do you think
I wouldn't fill volumes
About you
When you were gone?

An Unexpected Song

This song is a sound
you don't know you'd miss
until it's far away.
An opus of noise,
You can't tell if the notes are
At war or just at play.
The missed beats
And occasional harmonies
Form the background of each day.
This song is a sound
you don't know you'd miss
until it's far away.

With All

At what age do you know for sure
Life is going the way it should?
Looking out from this point, I see
Your own hand faint, but for my good.
On this still clings my timid hope
Under the weight of weariness:
Remember you know from the Lord
Help comes. But then I must confess
Each time my path presents me with
A new mountain for me to climb,
Resistance stalls my sullen steps;
To trudge with purpose takes me time.
So slowly I drag forward still,
Obeisance to the one I praise.
Unceasing, and to spite my will,
Love calls me upward through my days.
At times, I wonder why for me
No simpler roads will just appear.
I doubt that you have heard my cries.
I wonder if you've turned your ear.
I know, whatever I may say,
No matter, I still look to you. At times I wonder, and I pray
Do you love even me still too?

This might be wrong...

I yourself you.
But I can't
So you do
Through me.
A foolish and
Blasphemous
Notion I
pray you
Will forgive.

Don't miss out!

Visit the website below and you can sign up to receive emails whenever Wendelyn Vega publishes a new book. There's no charge and no obligation.

https://books2read.com/r/B-A-ORRF-SNBDD

BOOKS 2 READ

Connecting independent readers to independent writers.

Also by Wendelyn Vega

My Head Bowed: A Chapbook on Depression, Anxiety, and Faith
Kulebra
My Eyes Closed: A Chapbook on Identity, Grief, and Hope
Liani
My Heart Open

About the Author

Thank you for reading *My Heart Open: A Chapbook on Connection, Pain, and Love*! If you'd like to learn more about me or read my other work, visit my website at <u>WendelynVega.com</u>. Also, you can join my mailing list and get access to my freebie library at <u>books.wendelynvega.com</u>!

Wendelyn Vega is an author, poet, and international woman of timidity. She's also a language-enthusiast, fledgling artist, and constant daydreamer. When she's not writing, she enjoys reading, trying out new recipes, spending time with her husband, and playing with the three mini tigers she keeps in her house.

www.ingramcontent.com/pod-product-compliance
Lightning Source LLC
Chambersburg PA
CBHW030536080526
44585CB00014B/970